Stimulated by his sister Camille, Rodin's pupil, Claudel set off for the East. He spent the next twenty years in China and Japan in various diplomatic posts. There his ruminations about 'the sigu' in Chinese and Japanese writing, his contemplations of gardens and his interest in the meditations of monks all led to one result: a retreat into the self in a bitter-sweet circle.

These 'occidental ideograms' are some of Claudel's finest work, and were first published in 1927 in Tokyo. Long before the hai-ku was adopted by the 'Beat' poets of the sixties, he tried his own synthesis of this particular form. Claudel's poems of two or three short lines create an expressively poetic syllogism. By juxtaposing images, others, which are implicit, irresistibly spring to mind. They are printed here as he expressly stipulated in order to provoke a 'haemorrhage of the senses'. The idea of movement and its opposite, typified by a fluttering fan which suddenly clicks shut, often occurs in Claudel's work. From Taoist teaching he had learnt that 'immobility is not the privation of movement, but a movement free from local displacement'; a congenial notion for a man who had once wished to enter a contemplative Catholic monastery.

Together with his book, *Connaissance de l'Est*, this volume opened up new vistas for other French writers. Claudel expressed to his friend Mallarmé his sense of 'living in the most perfect oblivion which delights me'. These delicate, allusive verses are rooted in Claudel's very personal definition of that forgotten place.

Catholic, diplomat, dramatist and poet, Paul Claudel remains a *monstre sacré* of modern French literature. He was born in 1868 in a small village between the Ile-de-France and Champagne. He lost his faith and then regained it as the result of a mystical experience in Nôtre-Dame when he was eighteen, owed largely to his reading Rimbaud's *Les Illuminations*. For some years he attended Mallarmé's Symbolist salon in Paris, and discovered the literature that was to influence him most – the Bible, Aeschylus, Virgil and Dante. In 1893 he began his diplomatic career and was ambassador to America, China, Japan and Belgium. He died in 1955.

His plays include *The Satin Slipper*, *The Hostage* and *Break of Noon*. His poetic works include *Five Great Odes* and *Coronal*.

PAUL CLAUDEL

A Hundred Movements for a Fan

Translated from the French and with an
Introduction by ANDREW HARVEY & IAIN WATSON

QUARTET ENCOUNTERS

Quartet Books

This translation is dedicated to Meredith Etherington-Smith

First published in Great Britain
by Quartet Books Limited 1992
A member of the Namara Group
27/29 Goodge Street, London W1P 1FD

Originally published in French under the title
Cent phrases pour éventails in 1942

A catalogue record for this book is available from the
British Library

ISBN 0 7043 0175 X

Printed and bound in Great Britain by
BPCC Hazells Ltd
Member of BPCC Ltd

INTRODUCTION

The marvellously delicate and mysterious poems which the great French poet Paul Claudel finished in 1926 towards the end of his stay in Japan – *A Hundred Movements for a Fan* – are almost unknown outside France. They are amongst the most original works ever written by a westerner out of an exacting experience of the East.

A Hundred Movements for a Fan is the child of the marriage between Claudel's spirit and that of the traditional Japan he loved with amazement. In writing it, in Japan itself, Claudel did not surrender either his western identity or his peculiar preoccupations or his ingenuity or his integrity as a 'European' artist, but he allowed the spiritual delicacy of the Japanese vision to refine his own and transform his stormy and ebullient lyricism into something more graceful and poignant. The result is a work at once modern and ancient, western and eastern, hybrid and pure, hieratic and intensely intimate.

This translation was done over many years, as part of one westerner's practice of an eastern spiritual discipline. It has struggled to be as faithful to the turns and twists of the French original as possible, while also honouring the peculiar exigencies of English. Certain small changes in the layout of individual poems have had to be made.

In a text about *A Hundred Movements for a Fan* found among his papers, Claudel wrote:

> This book of poems where the author has tried to apply the principles of Japanese poetry – while transforming them to his own taste – is animated by the following ideas:
>
> Each poem is very short, only one phrase, enough, just, to support a breath – of sound, feeling, words – or the beating of the wing of a fan.

The actual 'writing' plays a large role in it, because in French as in Chinese the exterior form of letters is not foreign to the expression of an idea. A thousand secret intentions hide in the calligraphy operated by the brush of the poet himself . . .

What was intended through the disposition of lines and words, the interposing of white spaces, the suspension in the void of dead consonants, points and accents, the collaboration of meditation and expression, sound, voice, dream, memory, writing and thought, was that the intellectual vibration of each word or of the essential part of each word should reveal itself to a reader patient enough to savour each poem, one after the other, slowly, as you would drink a small cup of very hot tea.

Andrew Harvey & Iain Watson

AUTHOR'S PREFACE

It is impossible for a poet who has lived for some time in China and Japan to avoid thinking of using the paraphernalia which accompany their way of thought: first the stick of *encre de chine*, as black as our interior night; you rub it, moisten it slightly on a slate palette and a pot gathers the magic juice. What more need you do now, painter of ideas, but dip in the brush? That slender, almost aerial, brush which communicates along the joints of our fingers out of our depths up to the poem's conflagration. A few decided strokes, as sure as those an insect makes with its tererbra through the bark to paralyse its invisible prey – taking care only to roll up our sleeve and avoid that careless pinch of snuff in our nostrils that impeded the exhalation of the spirit – and here, in a few words, freed from the harness of syntax and joined once again by the whiteness of their simultaneity alone, a phrase made up of relations! Written on what? On the still red-hot belly, for example, of that piece of pottery just taken out of the kiln for us? Or – and this would be even better – on that wing that is the fan, entirely on the alert to propagate its breath. Accept then, in your heart's ear, that silent word dispatched by a breath born of a hand!

A Hundred Movements for a Fan. This is the group of poems ready today for the first time after sixteen years to fly away under our French sky, which, previously in Japan, looking for their shade, I rashly tried to mix in with the ritual swarm of the hai-ku.

What could have helped me to resist the omnipresent temptation over there of calligraphy? Not this brush already quivering at the end of my most relaxed fingers, and certainly not this proffered paper, as crackling as silk, as taut as a bow-string, as mellow as mist. Am I not too a writing specialist? As for western lettering, that which during the train of one's thoughts blends into words and letters, is it not in the gesture which links it to its neighbours something as animated, as peremptory, as the Chinese ideogram? In one movement, the character prints itself on the idea and offers it publicly and fixed in relation to the graphic constellation which it evokes all around itself. But the letter in its analysis and positioning on the horizontal line of the imaginary concept is at one and the same time a figure and a movement, a sort of semantic machine. 'O', depending on its linkage, can be the sun, the moon, a wheel, a pulley, an open mouth, a lake, a hole, an island, a zero – the function of all that. 'I' can be a dart, the pointed index finger, a tree, a column, the affirmation of personality and unity. 'M' is the sea, the mountain, the land, the measure, the soul, the identity. And if from all these mouths and added diagonal strokes we create a word, what more perfect ideogram than *heart, eye, sister, same, oneself, dream, foot, roof,* and so on? The word for us (which signifies *acquired by movement*) is a group formed by a succession. It goes on vibrating and emitting in that reining in of the whiteness, which contains it, the allure of the hand which formed it. You participate in the verve which welded the links of that chain. Sense travels always from left to right, and the hand, one line below the other, tirelessly accomplishes the same trajectory. The poet goes in his reader's direction, then turning back on himself, like the pen to the inkwell, starts the circuit afresh.

Only the paper is smooth, the letters, all of them inclining forwards, create a sort of slope which carries you along with it and soon the poet, unless he carefully controls his mount, that unbridled pen in his fingers, merely cares about the ending and not about the traces his gallop leaves behind him.

But if he had exchanged the pen for the brush, everything would have been different! A vertical care is substituted for the sloping yoke of three fingers and of style. In place of continuous vocalization, a letter-by-letter analysis. The word, deliberately drawn and perpendicular to the eye, gives off the entire sense of the diverse roles that it coagulates (and in the very word I have just written down does the ink not form in the reader's eyes a shining triple drop?) The poet is no longer simply the author, but the painter, spectator and critic of his own work, in as much as he sees it unrolling in front of him. His creation takes place under his eyes in slow motion. He has time. What need, then, for the exterior mechanical constraint of paper and prosody? Let us allow each word, whether of one or more vocables, each verbal proposition, the space – the time – necessary for its full sonority, for its dilation over the white space. May each group or graphic entity freely occupy in its given area the apt position which is fitting in its relation to other groups. Let us substitute for the uniform line an untrammelled delirium in the bosom of the second dimension! And, as it is thought alone which by a kind of ricochet solidifies the successive elements of the word, why not delay, when necessary, by a calculated spacing, the resolution of the black intellectual splotch, and so prolong the insistent appeal it articulates?

The poem itself is written in two parallel collumns, the margin being kept for what one might call a title, or derivation, or exclamation.

Brangues, 25 June 1941

A Hundred
Movements for a Fan

Tu   m'appelles   la   Rose
                          dit   la   Rose
          mais si tu savais
          mon vrai nom
          je m'   effeuillerais
                          aussitôt

Au   de la pivoine blanche
cœur   ce n'est pas une couleur
          mais le souvenir d'une
          couleur
          ce n'est pas une odeur
          mais le souvenir d'une
          odeu   r

You   *call me the Rose*
                       says the Rose
                but if you knew
                my real name
                I would   *shrivel*
                           at once

At the   *of the white peony*
heart   *is not a colour*
                but the memory of a
                colour
                is not a fragrance
                but the memory of a
                frag   *ra*   *nce*

Glycines

Il n'y aura jamais
assez de
fleurs pour nous empê
cher de comprendre ce
solide nœud de s
erpents

Glycines

Cèdre

Enlacé par
ses mille bras au
tronc du colosse fun
èbre   l'hydre
de la vie
escalade et remercie
la Mort

2

W*istaria*

There will never be
enough
flowers to prevent
us understanding this
solid knot of s
nakes

 W*istaria*

Cedar

Entwining with
its thousand arms the
trunk of the funereal col
ossus   the hydra
of life
clambers over and thanks
Death

J*izô*
sur
son
piédestal

ferme les yeux
comme un homme
en plein midi
qui ferme les yeux
à cause d'une lumière
trop grande[1]

U*ne*
pauvre
prière

fragile
comme une pierre
en équilibre
sur la tête
de
J*izô*

4

*Jizô
on
his
pedestal*

*closes his eyes
like a man
at full noon
from a too great
light*

*One
poor
prayer*

*fragile
as a stone
balancing
on the head
of
Jizô*

*C*omme
un
tisserand

par le moyen
de ma baguette
magique j'unis
un rais de soleil
avec un fil
de
pluie

O

tzuki sama[2]

Une grenouille saute
dans l'étang et là
haut dans le ciel

se met à rire si fort
qu'elle est obligée de
s'essuyer le coin de l'œil
avec un mouchoir de soie

*Like
a
weaver*

*by virtue of
my magic
rod I unite
a ray of sun
with a thread
of
rain*

---

*O

tzuki sama*

*A frog leaps
into the pond and there
high in the sky*

    *starts to laugh so loudly
it is compelled to
wipe the corner of its eye
with a silk handkerchief*

T*as*
de
pierres

sur la tête de
        Jizô
le dernier petit caillou
que ce ne soit pas
        un aveugle
qui soit chargé de le
        mettre

L*a*
nuit

approche ta joue
de ce bouddha de
pierre   et
ressens   combien
la journée a été
        brûlante

*H*eap
of
stones

on the head of
  Jizô
this last small pebble
let it not be
  a blind man
who is charged
  to place it

*N*ight

put your cheek close
to this buddha of
stone   and
                feel
how the day
  blazed

La journée
a été brûlante et
maintenant appr
oche
sens un dieu chaud

A*ppr*
oche

ton oreille et sens
combien au fond de la
poitrine d'un dieu
l'amour est long
à
s'éteindre

10

The day
blazed
and now appr
oaches
feeling a warm god

Place
your ear

close

and sense
how at the bottom
of the chest of a god
love is slow
to
die out

Dit Dieu

Ce n'est pas la
glycine
                    qui est
capable de me garrotter
        c'est la vigne
        et le raisin

*La
pivoine*

        et cette rougeur
        en nous
        qui précède
                la pensée

Says God   *It is not*
the wistaria
that can
garrot me
it's the vine
and grape

The
peony   *and this flush*
in us
that precedes
thought

13

Cette
nuit

il a plu

              du vin
Je le sais il n'y a pas
moyen d'empêcher les
roses de parler

Cette
nuit

     dans mon lit
    je vois que ma
       main
    trace une   o
mbre sur le mur
La lune   s'eſt levée[1]

To night   it rained
                                          wine
I know there was no
way to stop the
roses talking

To night   in my bed
                                 I see my
                                   hand
                       traces a shad
                   ow on the wall
              The moon   is   up

C_{ette}
o
    c

mbre que me confère
la lune
omme une
                  encre
immatérielle

J_e
suis
venu

     du bout du monde
pour savoir ce qui se
cache de rose au fond
des pivoines blanches
     de Hasédéra[1]

*T*his
  sh

  l

a dow that bestows
the moon
ike an   immaterial
      ink

I
have
come

from the ends of the earth
to know what of rose is
hiding at the heart
of the white peonies
of Hasedera

Rougeur

Le Sang
qui pénètre
la chair
et l'esprit
qui pénètre l'âme

---

*Seule
la
rose*

*est
assez fragile
pour exprimer
l'Éternité*

Redness   *Blood*
                            penetrating
                                flesh
                     spirit
                     penetrating soul

Only   *is*
the   *fragile enough*
rose   *to express*
                          Eternity

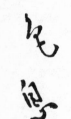

U*n*
certain
rose

qui eſt
moins une couleur
qu'une
respiration

U*ne*
odeur

que
pour sentir
il faut
fermer
*les y*ɩ*u*
x

20

A
certain
rose

less a
colour
than a
*   breath*

A
fragrance

*   that*
* to smell*
you have
* to close*
your eye
*   s*

雪
去

N ous
fermons les yeux
et la Rose dit
C'eſt
moi

旅
人

Voyageur !
approche
et respire enfin
cette odeu   r
qui guérit de tout
mouvement

W

       e
close our eyes
and the Rose says
       It is
         I

---

 *T*raveller

    !
     come
breathe in at last
this fragr   ance
that cures all
       movement

L_a
rose

n'est
que
la forme un instant tout
haut de ce que le cœur
tout bas appelle ses
délices

N_{ous}
r

ouvrons
les yeux
et la rose a   d
isparu   nous
avons tout   r
espiré

*T*he
rose

                                        nothing
                                          but
            the soaring transient form
            of what down below
            the heart calls its
                ecstasies

---

*W*e
  o

                                pen
                our eyes again
            and the rose has   dis
            appeared   we
                    breathed it
                    all in

25

Éventail

De la parole
du
poëte
il ne reste plus que le
S

ouffle

La
rose

J'ai franchi
sur un pont de corail
quelque chose qui ne
permet pas le retou
r

*F*an

Of the
      poet's
        word
there remains only the
        Br
          eath

---

*T*he
Rose

    I passed
on a bridge of coral
something that forbids
re
  turn

U_{ne}
rose

d'un rouge si fort
qu'elle tache
l'
â m e
comme du vin

U_{ne}
pivoine

aussi blanche
que le sang
est
rouge

28

A
rose

so strongly red
it stains the
s o u l
like wine

*P*eony

as white
as blood
is
red

La
neige

      sur
toute la terre
pour la neige
    étend
un tapis de
    neige

Au
travers
de
la
cascade

     une
longue fée horizontale
verte et rose
joue de la
    flût
    e

The
snow

over
the entire earth
unrolls
for the snow
a carpet of
snow

Through
the
water
fall

a
long horizontal
green and pink
fairy
plays the flu
te

Au
  son

                    de la flûte
                     d'argent
               se mêle une flûte
                       de
                    verr

                                    e

Moins

                 la rougeur
              de la pourpre
                que le s
                    on
                    de
                    l'
                    or

32

With the
sound
 of the silver
 flute
mingles a flute
 of
 glas   s

Less
 the redness
of purple
than the s
 ound
 of
 gold

Le
marcheur
solitaire

Pour ma bouche cette
poignée de cresson et
pour mes yeux tout là
haut au sommet de la
montagne cette tache
de neige   Trois
heures après midi

Comment
vous
parler
de
l'
automne

quand j'ai encore
dans l'oreille cette
aigre flûte du
*   printemps*
qui me remplit la bouche
*   d'eau*

Solitary
   walker

For my mouth
this handful of cress
for my eyes
up there at the top
of the mountain that smudge
of snow   Three
hours after noon

How
to speak
  to
  you
  of
autumn

when I have in
my ears still that
acrid spring
       flute
that fills my mouth with
        water

L'œil
sous la ligne déjà
déchiffre
une autre ligne

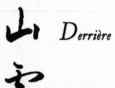 *Derrière*

la ligne
atramenteuse des
montagnes
il ne cesse de tonner
un tonnerre sombre

*T*he eye
beneath this line already
is picking out
another line

*B*ehind   the jagged line
of the
mountains
there never stops
growling dark thunder

*A*vant
   que
     le
 premier
  éclair

ne vienne prendre une
photographie génér
ale de toute la terre
        le lièvre
sur son autel de famille
allume une pastille
d'encen   *s*

L,
encen
  s

     comme ce vers
     que j'écris
     m
oitié cendre et moitié f
   umé   *e*

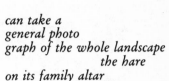

*B*efore   can take a
 the   general photo
 first   graph of the whole landscape
lightning   the hare
       on its family altar
        lights a stick
       of in cen se

---

*I*n   like this line
cen   I am writing
 se   ha
      lf ash half sm
       oke

*D*e l'   encen
                            s
                 il ne reste plus que la
                 fumé   e
                 de la fumée il ne reste
                 plus que l'odeu   r

---

*D*ans   sur une tombe
  la   abandonnée
  forêt   une lanterne
                  blanche

$O_{f\ the}$

incen
se
there remains   only
smo   ke
and of that
just this fragran ce

I_n
the
forest

on an abandoned
            grave
        a white
        lantern

Ah

le monde est si beau
qu'il faut poster ici que
lqu'un qui du matin au
soir soit capable de ne
pas remue
r

 Jizô[1]

Mettez
lui
deux cailloux sur la tête
il ne pourra pas
remue
r

42

O

the world is so
beautiful you should post here
someone who from dawn to
dusk need never
once
move

 Jizô

*Put
on his head
two pebbles
he can't
move*

Nuit

au sein de la
nuit
un aveugle
qui a envie de d
o
rmir

La
petite
maman

à
pas
vifs
enlève le cerf-volant
mais c'est l'enfant d
errière elle la bouche o
uverte
qui le fait voler

44

*N*ight

on the breast of
night
a blind man
who wants to sl
eep

---

*T*he
tiny
mother

with
rapid
steps
gets the kite off the ground
but it's the child behind
her with its mouth o
pen
that makes it   fly

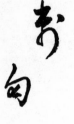

pas
mes
épines

qui me défendent
dit la Rose
c'est
mon parfu
m

Accroupi
près
du
bocal

Monsieur Chat
les yeux à demi fermés
dit
:
Je n'aime pas
le poisson

not   defend me
my   said the Rose
thorns   but
        my perfu
        me

Crouched   Sir Cat
by   eyes half-closed
the jar   says
           :
      I really don't like
      fish

Quand   ce petit enfant
je   dans mes bras
suis   il est juste assez lourd
à genoux   pour m'empêcher
     de
     me
     relever

Les   Et une épingle
deux mains   entre les dents
derrière   elle
la tête   regarde
     de côté

When   with this small child
  I'm   in my arms
kneeling   he's just heavy enough
              to stop me
                        get
                   ting   up

Her two hands   And a pin
    behind   between her teeth
  her head   she
              glances
                      sideways

Je salue
Monsieur Mon Enfant

L*e*
camélia
rouge

comme une idée
éclatante
et froide

50

I greet and honour
Sir My Child

*T*he
red
camellia

like a brilliant
and chill
idea

51

*U*n
rayon
de
soleil

dans un
tourbillon
de
neige

---

*L*e
camélia
panaché

une face rougeaude
de paysanne
que l'on voit à travers
la neige

52

A
ray
of
sun

in a
maelstrom
of
snow

---

*T*he
pied
camellia

a peasant woman's
ruddy face
glimpsed through
snow

*T*rébu
chant
sur mes
sandales
de bois

j'   essaye
d'   attraper
                            le
premier flocon de neige

*D*ans
la
lune
morte

Il y a
un lapin
vivant!

Stu
    mbling
in my   *I*   *try*
    wooden   *to*   *catch*
sandals   *the*
          first   *snowflake*

In
  the   *Look!*
  dead   *a rabbit*
  moon   *alive!*

*P*lus
d'
inspiration

le
poëte
pêche
sans hameçon
dans
une coupe de
saké

*D*es
deux
doigts

il soulève
la coupe
de saké
et ses lèvres
s'ouvrent
peu à peu

*N*o
*more
inspiration*

*the
poet fishes
without a hook
in
a cup of
sake*

---

*W*ith *just
two
fingers*

*he lifts up
the cup
of sake
and his lips
open
little by little*

Le
vieux
poëte

sent
peu à peu
un vers
qui le gagne
comme
un   éternuement

En
haut
de la
montagne

je suis venu
regarder
moins la mer
que
la cessation
de tout

58

The
old
poet

feels
a line
stealing up on him
slowly
like a sneeze

On
the
mountain-top

I came less
to   survey
the sea
than
the cessation
of everything

Au
point
du
jour

le Nantaï
au Shirane
décoche
une grande flèche
d'or[1]

Il
apparaît

un dieu
dans le brouillard
mêlé de
m orceaux d'or

*A*t
break of
day

the Nantaî
to Shirane
lets fly
a vast golden
arrow

*T*here
appears

a god
in the fog
mingled with
fl   ecks of   gold

Dans
le
brouillard

mêlé de
paillettes d'argent
l'ombre de la prêtresse
secouant son goupillon
de
g
relots et le semoir de son
s²

La
Prêtresse
du
Soleil

est assise
sur le plateau
d'une balance

62

In
the
fog

                    mingled with
                    silver grains
                    the priestess's shadow
                    shaking her aspergillum
                              of
                               b
                    ells and seed-bag of sound
                                              s

The
Priestess
of
the
Sun

                    is seated
                    on the pan
                    of a scale

Pour
adorer

le Soleil
Dieu
a mis
la Lune
à notre
disposition

 *Les premiers*
dieux

que la terre ait connus
étaient des espèces de
dieux paysans à tête de
chiens ou de lapins avec
des sarraux de toile
et de grosses chauss
ures de paille

To
adore

the Sun
God
has put
at our
disposal
the Moon

The first
gods

the earth ever knew were
sorts of God-peasants with
the heads of dogs or rabbits
canvas smocks and
big straw shoes

D'un
côté
du
lac

le Soleil Levant
et de l'autre côté
il arrive
un Serpent
à sept têtes

Je salue
en Monsieur Mon Enfant
Messieurs
les ancêtres
de mon mari

From one
side
of
the lake

the Rising Sun
and from the other
arrives
a Serpent
with seven heads

I greet and honour
in Sir My Child all
you Sir-
Ancestors
of my husband

Au centre

de
la grande Plaine
des Roseau
x

le Premier
Empereur
écoute
l'Empire

---

i

Vite
une   larme
qui
traverse
un rayon de soleil
elle a passé

At the centre

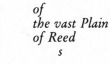

of
the vast Plain
of Reed
      s

the First
Emperor
listens to
the Empire

 i

Quick
a   tear
crossing
a ray of sun
it has gone

?

L'
Empereur Ermite
écoute
l'Empire
Tout à coup si la cascade
s'   arrêtait ?

E*ntre*

ce qui commence
et ce qui finit
l'œil du poëte a saisi cet
i
mperceptible poi
nt où quelque chose
p
ique

70

?

The
Hermit Emperor
listens to
the Empire
what if all at once
the waterfall
st   opped?

---

*B*etween

what begins
and what ends
the poet's eye has seized this
im
perceptible poi
nt where something
s
tings

71

Paravent

Tout commence
tout conspire
à l'or suprême

Toute
        la
nature

                sort de l'or
        elle émerge
        de son   bain
        d'éternité

*S*creen

Everything begins
everything conspires
to absolute gold

---

 *A*ll
Nature

arises from gold
emerges from
its bath of
eternity

K_{wannon}

Au bout de la baguette
devant l'autel de

ce point incandescent
qui eſt la frontière
entre la cendre
et le parfum

 J_e

conserverai
cette belle journée
sous les eaux
d'une laque
inaltérable

74

Kwannon

At the end of the rod
Before the altar of

this burning point
this frontier
between ash
and perfume

I

will preserve
this radiant day beneath
the waters
of lacquer
immovable

Éventail

Poëmes
é
crits sur le
s
ouffle

F in
d'août

Dans le brouillard
parmi des milliers de
libellules
trois
papillons blancs

*F*an

Poems
        wr
itten on the
br
        eath

E nd of
August

In the fog
among the thousands of
dragonflies
            three
        white butterflies

Celui qui ne

       regarde
   pas l'azalée
     n'entendra
       pas
      le
    t o r r e n t

Le
coucou

    localise
     l'endroit
     où nous ne
     sommes p
      as

*H*e who does   *gaze at*
not   *the azalea*
                       will not hear
                           the
                    s t r e a m

---

*T*he
cuckoo   *fixes*
                    the place
                    where we
                    are no   t

春秋

A l'un
des bouts
de ce
segment
de cercle

le printemps qui
commence
poursuit à l'autre bout
l'automne
également qui
commence

诗船

V oile

d'un petit bateau
dont la cargaison
est de quelques
syllabes

春
秋

At one
of the ends
of this
segment
of circle

the spring that is
beginning
chases to the other side
autumn
already begun

诗
船

Sail

of a small boat
whose cargo is
these few
syllables

Éventail

Ce ruban
demi-circulaire
eſt l'horizon
et la pointe du
triangle eſt l'
œil

J_e
tiens
l'
Année

dans ma main
il ne tient   qu'à moi
d'ouvrir d'un seul coup
avec gloire
les   XII   baguettes

F_{an}

This semi-circular
ribbon
is the horizon
and the point of the
triangle is the
eye

I
hold
the
Year

in my hand
it only remains   for me
to reveal with one sumptuous
gesture
the   XII   rods

Éventail

dans la main du p
oëte qui ordonne
la nature comme le
sextant du marin
calcule
le
      ciel

L'
automne

aussi
est une chose
qui
commence[1]

*F*_{an}

in the hand of the p
oet that regulates
nature like the
sailor's sextant
numbers
the

sky

*A*_u
tumn

also
is something
that
begins

*D*ialogue

de
l'éventail
avec
le
paravent

*É*ventail

Je
puise l'air
dans
un
pays
fitti
f

Dialogue

of
the fan
with
the
screen

Fan

I
fish up
the air
in
a
fictive
countr
y

Non pas
trois
mots noirs

sur une aile blanche
mais quelques m
iettes blanches
vers vous chassées
   par une aile
invisibl   e

En
hiver
un
instant

ce suspens
de cristal
et
voici que tout repart
à la fois comme une vitre
qu'on brise en mille
morceaux

*N*ot
three
black words

on a white wing
but some white cr
umbs driven towards you
  by this wing that's
invisibl   e

---

*I*n
winter
a
moment

this suspension
of crystal
and
everything falls apart at once
like a window
shattered in a thousand
  fragments

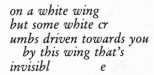

Les iris
pour
m'amener
jusqu'
ici

sont venus me rechercher
jusqu'aux portes de Tokyô
comme une
ribambelle de jeunes
paysannes entre les ros
eaux tout le long du f
ossé   plein

Les
iris

indéfiniment
sur la route comme les p
aysannes qui vont à la
foire   une
troupe jaune de temps en
temps après je ne sais c
ombien de troupes bleues

*T*he irises
to
lead me
here

came scouting for me
right up to the gates of Tokyo
like a
gaggle of young
peasant girls between the r
eeds all along the fu
ll   ditch

*T*he
irises

indefinitely
along the way like peasant
girls going to the
fair   one
yellow troupe from time to
time after I don't know how many
blue ones

J'
écoute

le torrent
qui se précipite
vers
sa
source

 L'
étoffe

du monde
depuis le temps qu'
elle sert comme c'est
curieux qu'il n'y ait pas
de
trou

I
listen

to
the stream
hurtling
towards
its
source

 This
cloth

the world's made of
how strange
it's been in use
all this time
and still hasn't
one
hole

*T*ant
de
choses
diverses

et
quand je ferme les yeux

je n'entends
plus que la seule rum
eur   du   torrent

---

*L*e
ruisseau
devant
et
derrière
moi

je cause à la fois
avec
tous les moments
de sa vie

So
many
different
things

yet
when I close my eyes

    I hear only
the single murmur
of the   stream

Stream
before
and behind
me

I am talking at the same
time with
all the moments
of its life

L'
idée
contre
l'idée

                                 la joue
                                 contre
                                 la joue

Au   *de la*   *forêt*
plus   *comme dans la pensée*
profond   *du vieux poëte*
                              s'est déclaré
            le   *mal*   *de*   *l'or*

*I*dea
against
idea

cheek
against
cheek

*I*n the
furthest
depths

of the   forest
as in the thought
of the old poet
            spoke out
the evil of gold

*D*ans
la
noirceur

immobile
de la verdure
le rugissement
de   la   pourpre

---

*E*ntre
le
jour
et la
nuit

ce n'eſt pas encore
aujourd'hui
c'eſt   hier

98

In
the
immobile

blackness
of the verdure
the groaning
of purple

Between
day
and
night

it isn't yet
today
it is   yesterday

Chut !

        si nous
faisons du bruit
     le temps
va recommencer

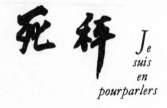

*J*_{*e*}
suis
en
pourparlers

    avec la mort
    je pèse
ses propositions

*Q*uiet!

make one sound
and time
begins again

I am
dealing
with
death

weighing
its
propositions

*U*ne
belle journée
d'automne

eſt comme la
vision
de   la   Juſtice

---

*F*enêtre

au lever du soleil
qui s'o   uvre dan
s le bro   uillard
b l a n   c un pay
s de braise et de
            fe
            u

O*ne*
radiant autumn
          day   *is like the*
                                          vision
                                    of   Justice

W*indow*   *at daybreak*
                open   ing into the white
                m   ist country of ember
                                    and
                                     fi
                                     re

L_e
Cèdre
et la
G
lycine

Hercule
et
l'   Hydre
au
Jardin des Hespérides[1]

U_n
fût

énorme et pur qui se d
érobe aussitôt au sein d'
un noir feuillage
Kwannon
au temple de Hasé dont
on ne voit que les pieds d'or

104

Cedar
and
W
istaria

Hercules
and
the   Hydra
in the
Garden of the Hesperides

A
pure
and
vast
column

vanishing at once
in the bosom
of dark foliage
            Kwannon
in the temple of Hase
where you see only
her golden feet

C*èdre*

Je gémis
au pied
d'une tour
inaccessible

U*n poëme*

q
ui roule de tous côtés
sur le papier sans pouv
oir s'y fixer comme une
g
outte d'eau sur une feui
lle de lotus

C*edar*

I groan
at the foot
of an inaccessible
tower

P*oem*

r
olling from side
to side
on the paper un
able to settle
like a dr
op of water on a lo
tus leaf

Il faut

qu'il y ait
dans le poëme
un nombre
tel
qu'il empêche
de compter

Brûlure
en
moi

de cette douleur
qui essaye
vainement
de redevenir
une parole

*I*n a
poem

there must be
a number
that
stops it ever
being counted

---

*T*his
burning
in
me

of that grief
struggling
futilely
to become again
a word

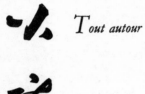 _Tout autour_

　　　　　　du poëme
　　　　d'autres petits poëmes
　　　　　　à moitié nés
　　　dont il n'est sorti qu'
　　　un adjectif ou une
　　　　　　　m
　　　　　ajuscule

 _Au_
centre

　　　　de la pivoine
　　　une abeille noire
　　　qui rentre et ressort
　　　avec volupté　　le
　　　dard suprême de s
　　　on corselet

110

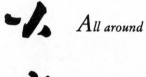

*A*ll around   the poem
other small poems
half-born
with only an adj
ective or a capit
al letter
yet emerged

*A*t the   of the peony
heart   a black bee
putting in and out
voluptuously   the
supreme sting of i
ts corselet

Cette
abeille

qui se meurt d'
amour au centre
de la rose si tu la t
ouchais quelle piq
ûre   !

Aucun
nombre

mais
une odeur
indivisible

This
bee

dying of love at
the heart of the
rose if you touched
it how it would st
ing   !

No
number

but an
indivisible
fragrance

*E*_{ncre}

sève
de l'esprit
et sang
de la pensée

---

*Q*ue
le
souffle

de l'éventail
disperse les mots
et ne laisse passer
que ce qui
touche

*I*nk

sap
of spirit
blood
of thought

---

*M*ay
the
breath

of this fan
scatter these words
and let pass only
those that
touch

*P*ar
toutes
les
routes

autour de Tokyô
les Iris
se sont mis en marche
pour aller voir
l'Empereur

*L*e
Fouji

L'Ange
du Japon
a revêtu son surplis
de plumes

116

On
all
the
roads

around Tokyo
the Irises
have started walking
to see
the Emperor

Fuji

the Angel
of Japan
has put on again
its cass
ock of feathers

117

L*e*
Fouji

à une hauteur
incommensurable
comme le trône de
Dieu s'avance
vers nous porté sur
une mer de nuages

L*e*
Fouji

là-haut au-dessus
des montagnes ap
paraît tout de neige
dans le ciel glacé
tandis qu'à droite et
à gauche et au-dessous
en énormes rouleaux
se retire la matière Olympienne

*F*_{uji}

at an immeasurable height
like the throne of
God   comes towards
us   carried
on a sea of clouds

---

  *F*_{uji}

up there above
the mountains appears
all of snow in a heaven
of ice while to
right and left and
below on enormous rollers
Olympian matter draws back

*Quatre
heures
du
matin*

*La couleur et la
lumière   le soleil
et la lune   se
mêlent   comme
l'eau avec le vin*

---

*Quatre
heures
du
soir*

*Semence de la nuit
la Lune
au ciel
accroît peu à peu
sa lumière*

120

Four
in the
morning

Colour and light
sun and moon
mingle   like
water and wine

Four
in the
evening

The night sows its seed
little by little
the moon in the sky
gathers light

*S*ous
les
pieds
de
la
Lune

d'un bout de la
terre à l'autre
un
chemin
de
sommeil

*C*omprends

cette parole
à l'oreille
de ton âme
qui ne résonne
que parce qu'elle a
cessé

Under
the
feet
of
the
moon

from one end of
the earth
to
the other
a road
of sleep

Understand

that word
at the ear
of your soul
which rings only
because it is
over

J'*écoute*

à mon oreille
la voix
de quelqu'un
qui parle
les yeux fermés

R*ide*

L'eau
que touche
l'idée

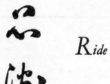

*L*istening

someone's
talking to me
with his eyes
closed

*W*rinkle

Water
touching
idea

Lève-toi

    assez   tôt
       pour
du festin mystérieux
  de la nuit
recueillir ces quelques
m i e t t e s

J'ai

   aux poissons
     muets
   émietté
ces quelques paroles
     sans
         bruit

*G*et up   *early   enough*
             to
     recover from night's
     mysterious feast
        these few
       c r u m b s

I have   *crumbled for the silent*
                  fish
   this handful of words
      without
           sound

*P*_{*our*}
donner

au riz
sa saveur
un petit bout
de
navet confit

Une
prune   salée
recrée
le
r i z

*T*o *give*

rice
savour
a sliver
of
pickled turnip

One
salted   prune
and the rice
tastes
fresh

129

Cette
fleur
jaune
et
blanche

comme
un
mélange
de feu   et de
lumière

Le
Japon

comme un long
Kotô
tout entier
a frémi sous le doigt
du Soleil Levant

This
yellow
and white
flower

like
a
mingling
of fire and
light

Japan

like a long
Koto
trembled
down its entire length
under the finger
of the Rising Sun

*C*reuse

ce jardin
comme une tasse
où tu viendras goûter
l'élixir
de tout ce paysage
aromatique

L'amour
et
l'encens

A ce point
brûlant
a succédé
une
odeur invincible

*E*mpty

this garden
like a cup you will
come to taste
the elixir
of all this aromatic
landscape

---

*L*ove
and
incense

*After long
burning
invincible
fragrance*

*Avec
une
brique*

*j'ai essayé
de me défendre
contre la
mouche à feu*

*J'ai
respiré*

*le paysage
et maintenant
pour dessiner
je retiens mon souffle*

134

With
a
brick

I tried
to defend myself
against the
firefly

I breathed
in

the landscape
now
to draw it
I hold my breath

G*uéri*
       de la mer
       j'offre en ex-voto
       une ancre
       toute rouillée et incrustée
       de coquilles

L*es*
îles
       autour de moi
       comme ces blocs de
       liège qui servent à
       retenir le filet

       La Lune
       est prise

136

*C*ured

> of the sea
> I offer as an ex-voto
> an anchor
> rusted all over and encrusted
> with shells

---

*I*slands

> around me
> like those chunks of cork
> keeping the net in place
>
> The Moon
> is taken

*A* la
fatale
trompette

notre âme
n'a pas encore
appris l' art
de rester
sourde

*J*e
danse

sur le monde
et frappe la terre
sous mes pas
d'un pied
alternativement
retentissant et muet

At
the fatal
trumpet

our soul
still will not know
how to stay
deaf

I
dance

on the world
and drum the earth
under my feet
alternately
thunderous and silent

*L*a
danse

du   printemps
de plus en plus vite
à la mesure des choses
qui croissent et se
m
u l ti p l i e n t

*E*ncre

Joie
du
jus
noir

140

*T*he
dance

of   spring
faster and faster
to the rhythm of
things burgeoning
and p r o
l i f e r a t i n g

*I*nk

Joy
of
black
sap

L'
encre

n'est
que
de l'or
concentré

La
rivière
sous
les
feuilles

Pendant que je peins
j'entends
un bruit d'or

142

The
ink

       is
    only
    gold
concentrated

River
under
the
leaves

while I paint
  I hear
a rush of gold

*L*a
nature

en grands vers
articule un texte
solennel
et
douloureux

L'Arbre
de
la
Chair

pareil
à un monſtrueux
cerisier
aux ventouses roses
et aux boutons
d'un violet virulent

Nature

in sweeping lines
articulates
a text
anguishing
and
solemn

*The Tree
of the
Flesh*

like
a monstrous
cherry-tree
with pink suckers
buds of virulent violet

Une
vapeur
d'or

réunit tout le paysage
dans le bain d'une ant
iquité immémoriale
joie nouvelle
et l'éternelle splendeu
r

Bruit

de l'eau
sur de l'eau
ombre
d'une feuille
sur
une autre feuille

146

A
steam
of gold

absorbs the whole landscape
into a bath of immemorial
ancientness fresh
ecstasy
of the eternal splendou
r

*N*oise

of water
on water
shadow
of a leaf
on
another leaf

*L*a
pluie

peu   à   peu
devient de la neige
la boue
peu   à   peu
devient de l'or

*D*ans
une écuelle
de terre

je bois
une gorgée
de sève

*R*ain

    little   by   little
      becomes snow
         mud
    little   by   little
      becomes gold

*I*n
a bowl
of earth

    I drink
   a draught
    of sap

*A*près
un
long
voyage

on me présente à un vi
eux cerisier tel qu'un
vieillard démantelé
dont la bénédiction
m'était indispensable

*T*emple

Il se passe
quelque chose dans l'
ombre   et
tout à coup une flamme
s'allume
dans le miroir d'argent

*A*fter
 a
 long
 journey

I am presented to an anc
ient cherry-tree like
a skeletal old man
whose blessing
was indispensable

*T*emple

Something
happens in the sh
adow   sud
denly a flame
flares
in the silver mirror

Départ

La   g
outte d' eau
            à
l'extrémité de cette
aiguille de pin
prête à se réunir à la
mer   tremble
        hésite

Sur
une
planche

        au milieu
des champs de riz
    je   traverse
    une   rivière
        rapide
        et
        trouble

Departure

        The   dr
      op of water
          at
            the very tip of this
        pine needle
ready to merge again with the
sea   trembles
        hesitates

On
a
plank

      in the middle
of the paddy-fields
I   cross   a
     rapid
     wild
     river

L*e*
souvenir
déjà

se mêle
à
la
fumé   e
bleu   e
de   Kyotô

U*n*
pin
la
mer
il
a
plu

Loin
de tout regard humain
la mer
est occupée
à faire le siège   *d'*
une goutte
d'
eau

*A*lready   is mingling
   the   with
   memory   the
                    bl   ue
                    sm   oke
                    of   Kyoto

---

*P*ine   Far
            from all human eyes
sea   the sea
                is busy
after   besieging   a
rain   drop
                  of
                    water

I*l*
   a
plu

            un rayon
          de soleil
   le lac   reflète
          un
         pin
     tout revêtu
   de gouttes d'eau

É*ventail*

       c'est l'espace
lui-même en se repliant
qui absorbe

          cet oiseau
immobile à tire d'aile
         s

*A*fter   a ray
rain   of sun
          the lake   reflects
                a
              pine
            swaddled
        with drops of water

---

*F*an   space
        bending back on itself
        that absorbs
            this immobile bird
                fast

*S*ur
l'eau
brune
et
trouble

un
duvet
de
canard

*N*on

Non
une cloche
au fond de moi-même
a   vibré
entre une quadruple
paroi

*O*n
the
brown
shaken
water

a
down
of
ducks

*N*o

No
a bell
in my deepest self
quivered
between a four-sided
wall

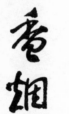

O_{ui}

O_{ui}
de l'autel
entre les arbres
s'élève
la fumé e
du sacrifice

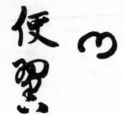

C'est le messager
qui arrive
avec ses deux ailes

160

*Y*es

Yes
from the altar
between the trees
rises
the smok e of
the sacrifice

The two-win
ged mess
en ger
arriving

Œil
oreille

                   mots
mouillés
    dont la secrète
sensibilité
       a pour centre
une goutte d'eau

L'
automne

         Au-dessus
du ruisseau clair et vif
    une touffe
     de chrysanthèmes
          jaunes

162

*E*ye
ear

              sodden
words
       whose secret
tenderness
       has at heart
a drop of water

*A*utumn

     Below
the quick clear stream
    a tuft
of yellow chrysanthemums

Apprends

que   l'or
peut   être
doux
comme
le   lait

La
goutte
d'
eau

sent
que toute la mer
est occupée
à
la solliciter

Learn   that   gold
                           can   be
                           tender
                             as
                             milk

The   *feels*
drop   *the entire sea*
of   *busy*
water   *tempting it*

La rose
est plantée dans
la terre
et le chrysanthème
est cultivé
dans le brouillard

*V*erse

un vin pur
et
un or
intellectuel

166

The rose
is planted in
    earth
the chrysanthemum
        grown
in fog

Pour

a pure wine
    and
intellectual
    gold

Entre
  ces
paupières

qui s'ouvrent
    deux
gouttes d'eau
  à la fois

Dieu
une seconde
a trouvé
cette goutte d'eau
au fond de mon
âme

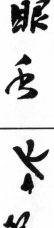

*B*etween
these
eyelids

that open
two
drops of water
at once

God
another also
has found
this drop of water
at the bottom of my
soul

Le
miroir
Shintô

Le temple
qui s'ouvre
laisse voir
une goutte d'eau
dans ses
profondeurs[1]

Si l'on veut
me séparer du Japon
que ce soit
avec une poussière
d'
or

170

神鏡

The mirror
Shinto

The temple
opening
to reveal
a drop of water
in its
depths

別

If I am to be
separated from Japan
let it be
with a dust
of
gold

離